Stars at Night

To Bethany, Beth, Rebecca, Charley and Rory

Published by
The Bible Reading Fellowship
Peter's Way, Sandy Lane West
Oxford OX4 5HG
ISBN 1 84101 101 0

First edition 2000
10 9 8 7 6 5 4 3 2 1 0

Acknowledgments
Scripture quotations are taken from the Good News Bible
published by The Bible Societies/HarperCollins*Publishers* Ltd UK
© American Bible Society, 1966, 1971, 1976, 1992.

A catalogue record for this book is available from the British Library.

Printed and bound in Great Britain by Caledonian International
Book Manufacturing Ltd, Glasgow.

Beginning with God

Stars at Night

Exploring the Bible with 5-7s

Rachel Heathfield

A note to parents and carers

This material is to be used ideally with some help. It is designed to help you to talk to your child about God-things and to learn together.

Every session begins with an idea for looking back at the day and thinking of something or someone in particular. That thing or person is then to be prayed for. Encourage your child to voice their prayer, even if it is just a name or word.

The next bit is to enable you to talk together about a topic which will help you to understand what the Bible verse of the day is about. There are no right or wrong answers here, simply ideas to get you thinking on the right lines. Do not be afraid of difficult questions your child might raise; just be as honest as you can.

There is always a suggestion of something to do, which varies from matching up pictures to organizing a time to get up and see the sunrise. This section is deliberately worded so that the activity doesn't have to happen at that moment—particularly if you do the sessions at bed-time! Please support your child by helping him or her to do the activity, and give a reminder of why that activity was suggested.

Explore the Bible is designed to bring together the talking and doing you have just worked through. It might raise more questions, and the answers should be made easier by referring back to the talking bit.

The last part of the session is for the child to complete their own prayer journal on the pages provided. Each session has a linked thought and prayer suggestion. Again, this can be completed straightaway or at another time. Some children might need help; others might like to do it on their own.

I hope you enjoy this material, and may God bless the time you spend with your child exploring the Bible together.

Rachel Heathfield

Who's coming?

Looking back

Think about your day just gone.

Think of something brilliant. Why was it good?

Say thank you to God!

To talk about

Where in your house is dark? Under the stairs, under your duvet? Where else?

Where does light come from in your house? Think of as many light sources as you can.

If you were to look outside in the daytime, where does the light come from?

Which lights are small, which are big?

Explore the Bible

> **The people who walked in darkness have seen a great light. They lived in a land of shadows, but now light is shining on them.**
>
> *Isaiah 9:2*

This verse says that the people couldn't see how God wanted them to live. It was as if they were in darkness, unable to see properly. God knew, so he sent them a light to help them see properly. It was a great light and it wasn't a 'what', it was a 'who'! Let's find out who is God's great light.

To do

Find a light that you can shine somewhere dark. How about a torch under your duvet?

What difference does the light make?

Which of these makes a great light?

Prayer jotter

Sometimes, understanding or doing difficult things is a bit like being in the dark. God wants to shine his light for us.

Do you need help with something you find difficult? Draw or write about it and ask God for his light to help.

Who's the child?

Looking back

Think of your day just gone.

Did you do or say anything that upset someone else or God?

Do you need to say sorry to that person?

Say sorry to God.

To talk about

From where you sit now, can you see anything with a label on it? A game, your clothes or a packet of food? What does the label tell us?

What do you know that has a sign on it? Your street or house? What do the roadside signposts tell us?

Do people ever describe you with a label? Tall, funny, gorgeous, lovely?

What do people call you? What does it mean?

To do

When you go out today or tomorrow, look for signs and labels. What do they tell us about things?

Look at these labels. What do you think would be on them—a picture or words?

Explore the Bible

In the last session, we saw that God was sending a great light—a light that was a 'who'.

These verses are like a signpost that helps us to see who is coming.

> **A child is born to us! A son is given to us! And he will be our ruler. He will be called, 'Wonderful Counsellor', 'Mighty God', 'Eternal Father', 'Prince of Peace'.**
>
> *Isaiah 9:6*

The great light is to be a child! And this child will have special names. Look at the verse—what are those names? The names help us to understand who this child will be. They are words a bit like a label, that describe what he will be like.

Prayer jotter

When we pray, we are talking to someone with all these special names.

What special names would you use when you talk to God? Write a prayer using your special name for God or draw a picture for him.

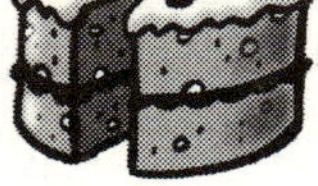

Immanuel

Looking back

Think of your day just gone. What made you feel happy? Say thank you to God.

To talk about

What is the best present you have ever been given? What made it so good? How did you feel when you got it?

How does it feel to get Christmas presents ready to give? Why do we give people presents?

To do

Make some tree decorations from card and ribbon some time between now and Christmas.

Here are some for you to copy. They will be a reminder that the best Christmas present ever was Jesus.

Explore the Bible

Do you remember the great light God was sending? Do you remember the descriptions of the child? Look back if you need to!

Today we see another description, a very special name for the child—Immanuel.

> **The Lord himself will give you a sign: a young woman who is pregnant will have a son and will name him 'Immanuel'.**
>
> *Isaiah 7:14*

These verses were written many years before Jesus was born.

The name Immanuel means 'God is with us' and is another name for Jesus. We see this name again in Matthew 1:22 and 23, some of the verses of the Christmas story.

Jesus being born is like an amazing present from God himself! Immanuel is the name that reminds us that Jesus is God's gift to us! Fill in your own name on the label.

Prayer jotter

A present always cheers us up. Is there anyone you know who needs to be cheered up by knowing that God is with them? Write a prayer for them or draw a picture of them getting a present.

How can *you* show them that God is with them (Immanuel)? Ask God to help you.

The real light

Looking back

Think about the people you know.

Is there anyone who needs to know God's love? Who? Why?

Pray for that person.

To talk about

When you begin to get excited about Christmas, what are you most looking forward to? Presents? Parties? No school? Having fun with family and friends?

One of the best things about presents is trying to guess what they are, even though they are wrapped up. Do you get excited by trying to guess?

To do

Guess what is inside these presents.

Explore the Bible

In the last session, we saw that Jesus coming as a baby at Christmas was like a present from God.

Today we are reminded that the people in the Bible were waiting for a great light.

> **This was the real light—the light that comes into the world and shines on everyone.**
>
> *John 1:9*

This real light was Jesus. Here we see that he was coming to bring light to shine on everyone. Seeing a light cheers us up and helps us to do things properly—this is what Jesus does for people, both then and now.

Prayer jotter

Think about Jesus being the real light in the world. Is there anywhere that you can think of, near to you or far away, that needs to see Jesus' light? Think of other children around the world who might be in a country at war or might be hungry.

Write or draw a prayer for them.

Full up

Looking back

Did you fall out with anyone in the day just gone? With friends? With those at home?

Does anything need sorting out? Do you need to say sorry?

Say sorry to God and ask him to help you sort things out.

To talk about

What is the difference between something that is full and something that is empty? Can you see anything that is full from where you are now? A glass? A box? A cupboard?

When something is full, we usually say what it is full of—a glass of water, a box of toys, a cupboard of clothes.

Sometimes, people are described as being full of something. Perhaps they are full of fun or full of laughter. Have you ever heard that said? Have you ever been described like that?

To do

Think about your friends and family. How would people describe each of them?

Full of… what?

Explore the Bible

The Word became a human being and, full of grace and truth, lived among us. We saw his glory, the glory which he received as the Father's only Son.

John 1:14

When Jesus came to earth, he came as a proper human being. This verse has yet another name for Jesus—the Word. But Jesus was a very special human, because he was full of God. The verse says he was 'full of grace and truth' and that we 'saw his glory'—he was a human so full of God that everyone saw he was different. Everyone saw that he was special.

Prayer jotter

When we know God for ourselves, we are full up too! The Holy Spirit lives in us and helps us to be like Jesus.

Write or draw about being full up with God.

Say a prayer thanking God that he fills you with his Holy Spirit.

Who's coming again?

Looking back

Think about your day just gone.

Have you done anything new today?

Something at school? Outside? At home?

Thank God for what you can do.

To talk about

What do you do when you are expecting someone to visit you? Tidy up? Help get some food ready?

Have you ever not been ready when someone came to visit? Perhaps they were early, or were they a surprise?

Was the house ready? What about you—were you ready?

How did it feel if you weren't ready?

To do

Think of a really special person—perhaps someone on television or a member of the royal family, perhaps your grandparents…

Pretend that the really special person is coming to your house.

What do you need to get ready?

Look at these pictures. Put a circle around the things to keep in order to be ready for a guest, and cross out the things to get rid of.

Explore the Bible

During Advent, the weeks before Christmas, we remember Jesus coming to be with us. But that was only the first time he came! He has promised to come back a second time. Look out for yet another name for Jesus!

> **'So then, you also must always be ready, because the Son of Man will come at an hour when you are not expecting him.'**
>
> *Matthew 24:44*

Just as we get our homes ready for a visitor, so we should always be ready for Jesus to come again. But is it our homes that need to be ready for Jesus, or is it something else?

Prayer jotter

Jesus will come for a second time when we don't expect him.

Jesus won't really mind about our houses being tidy but he will look into our lives and hearts. Is yours ready?

Write or draw a prayer asking God to help you be ready for him.

A baby is due

Looking back

Think of your favourite people.

Thank God for what you like about them.

Ask God to be with lonely people.

To talk about

Do you know anyone who is having or who has just had a baby?

Are they excited about it? What preparation do you have to make for a baby coming?

What does a mum have to think about?

To do

Circle the things you would need in preparation for a new baby.

Explore the Bible

> **God sent the angel Gabriel to a town in Galilee named Nazareth. He had a message for a young woman named Mary. The angel said, 'You will become pregnant and give birth to a son, and you will name him Jesus.'**
>
> *Luke 1:26–31*

Mums usually find out that they are having a baby by going to the doctor's and the hospital. Mary found out from an angel! How do you think she felt when she heard the news? It wasn't just the way she heard the news that shocked Mary, there was something else shocking, too.

Mary must have felt frightened and happy at the same time when she heard about the baby.

Prayer jotter

For most people, having a baby is happy news, but for some people the news is very scary.

Write a prayer here for all the mums in the world. Or draw a picture prayer about them.

What is impossible?

Looking back

What was really fun today? Thank God for it!

What made you sad? Tell God about it!

To talk about

What do you know is impossible to do?

Pour a jug of water into an egg-cup?

Light a candle without a match?

Paint a picture of sand and sea with only yellow paint?

Do you think it is possible or impossible to have a baby without a mummy and a daddy?

To do

Look at these things. Which things for you are impossible?

Which are possible? Which might seem hard but with practice might become possible?

Explore the Bible

Mary said, 'I am a virgin. How, then, can this be?' The angel answered, 'The Holy Spirit will come on you, and God's power will rest upon you. The child will be called the Son of God. For there is nothing that God cannot do.'

Luke 1:34–35, 37

Mary was shocked at the idea of having a baby. She and Joseph weren't yet married and Mary knew that it was impossible to have a baby if there is a mum but no dad.

But the angel's reply told her that God's Holy Spirit would make it possible for Mary to be the mother of God's own son—an amazing miracle that would never happen again. *Nothing* is impossible for God!

Prayer jotter

Are there things that feel impossible to you? Do you need God to help you practise to make them possible?

Maybe you need God's help to accept that you'll never be able to do some things.

Write or draw about it here.

Be brave, Joseph!

Looking back

Do you know of any places in the world where people are suffering at the moment?

Ask God to give them what they need.

To talk about

Have you ever wanted to do something but had second thoughts because it looked too difficult?

How about getting across a big climbing-frame? Or picking up a more difficult reading book? What about talking to a new person at school or a club you go to?

Did you manage to do any of the difficult things you thought of?

What was it like to be brave?

To do

Which of these things do you need to be brave for?

Explore the Bible

> **An angel of the Lord appeared to Joseph and said, 'Do not be afraid to take Mary to be your wife. She will have a son, and you will name him Jesus.'**
>
> *Matthew 1:20 and 21*

Mary and Joseph weren't married when Mary found out that she was having a baby. Joseph knew that other people might be rude or say mean things because of it. He was confused about what to do. The angel told him not to be afraid to marry Mary as planned. Joseph needed God's help to be brave. He knew that with God, everything would be OK.

Prayer jotter

Joseph needed God's help to be brave.

What do you need to be brave about? Tell God about it and ask him to help you.

Write a prayer or draw about being brave.

The royal baby

Looking back

Have you done anything in the day just gone that wasn't nice?

Say sorry to God.

Ask God to help you not to do it again.

To talk about

Imagine what it's like to be a king or queen. What clothes would you wear? What would your palace be like? What food would you eat? How would you spend your days?

If a royal baby was born, what would it have?

To do

Jesus was a baby born to be king. But what things did he have?

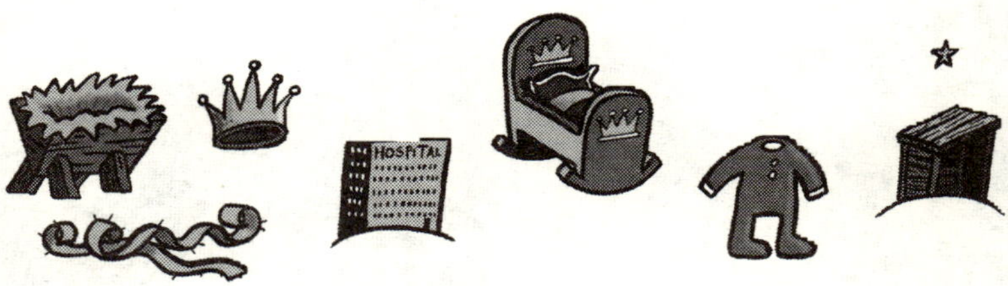

Explore the Bible

Joseph went from Nazareth to Bethlehem. He went with Mary. While they were in Bethlehem she gave birth to her first son, wrapped him in strips of cloth and laid him in a manger—there was no room for them to stay in the inn.

Luke 2:4–7

In the first few pages of this book, we found out about who the people were waiting for—a king, a light, a gift from God. And here he was! He had arrived, born as a baby in a little shed in Bethlehem. Not a very grand beginning for a king!

But this king wasn't going to be king of a country; he was going to be the king of heaven.

Prayer jotter

What does heaven look like?

Are you one of the people who is going to be living there?

Draw a picture or write some words about Jesus, the king of heaven.

Lights and music

Looking back

What was the weather like in the day just gone?

God made the weather—thank him, whatever it was like.

To talk about

What is the brightest light you have ever seen? A stage light? Or maybe you've seen a lighthouse?

Imagine a light much, much brighter.

What is the most beautiful music you have ever heard? On a CD or maybe in a church or cathedral or at a concert?

Imagine music more beautiful than that.

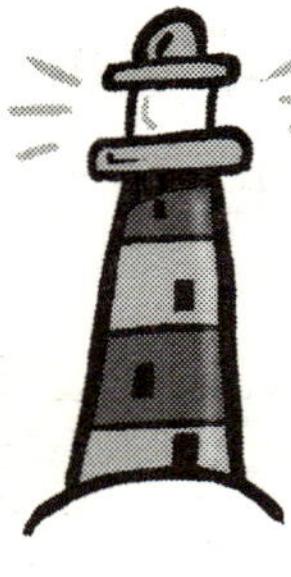

To do

Close your eyes and imagine sitting on a hilltop at night.

All you can see is a few stars. You can hear a few sheep bleating in the distance.

Suddenly, the sky is brilliantly bright and the air is full of music.

How do you feel?

Explore the Bible

> **There were some shepherds in that part of the country. An angel appeared and said, 'This day your Saviour was born—Christ the Lord.'**
>
> *Luke 2:8–11*

The shepherds must have been frightened and amazed at the same time. We read in the Bible (look up the verses that follow these ones if you can) that the sky was filled with angels—not just one, as Mary and Joseph had seen—but thousands!

The message was so important and exciting—Jesus had been born! Fantastic!

Prayer jotter

Can you imagine singing a song of praise to God like the angels did?

They were celebrating Jesus being born.

Write a song or poem about Jesus' birth or draw the angels singing.

Amazing facts

Looking back

Where are you now? What is comfortable? What you sit on? Your clothes?

Thank God for his care for you.

Pray for those people without a home and with very few clothes.

To talk about

Have you found out any amazing facts recently?

Maybe a huge number, or maybe an amazing fact about the world.

Can you remember how it felt to try to understand what that fact was all about?

To do

Here are some amazing facts.

- A star's temperature is 16,000,000 °C—that's very hot!
- To get to the sun in a car would take you 50 million years—that's very long!
- The moon is 3476 km in diameter—that's very wide!

Explore the Bible

The shepherds hurried off and found Mary and Joseph and saw the baby lying in the manger. The shepherds told them what the angel had said about the child. All who heard it were amazed at what the shepherds said.

Luke 2:16–18

The shepherds heard the angel's message and hurried to see for themselves. They were so amazed to have been told about the baby—that he was to be a king—that they were bursting to tell people! Everyone they told was also amazed.

Prayer jotter

The world is amazing. Our bodies are amazing.

God designed and made them all.

Thank God in a prayer or a picture for the things you find amazing.

Follow the star

Looking back

In the day just gone, have you seen or met someone who was sad?

Ask that God will make it possible for them to be happy again.

To do

What do these signs mean?

To talk about

Have you ever seen a sign and not understood it? What did you do?

Explore the Bible

> **Some men who studied the stars came from the east to Jerusalem and asked, 'Where is the baby born to be the king of the Jews? We saw his star when it came up in the east, and we have come to worship him.'**
>
> *Matthew 2:1–2*

The men who studied the stars were very wise. In those days, if people didn't understand something, they probably asked these men. The wise men had seen a new star in the sky and understood it to be a sign that a new king was born. They didn't waste time and came to meet him straightaway.

Prayer jotter

When it is a starry, clear night, do you ever look up and see patterns in the stars? God is so clever that he even knows the stars by name. Imagine how many names he needs!

Say a ‘thank you’ prayer to God and draw a starry night.

Gifts

Looking back

In the day just gone, was there anything your head told you to do because it was the right thing, but that you ignored, so that you ended up doing the wrong thing?

That makes God sad. Say sorry to him now.

To talk about

If you were going to see a new baby, what presents would you take?

Would you take anything for the baby's mum?

Have you seen a new baby? What are they like? What do they do?

To do

Which of these presents is good for a baby?

Explore the Bible

When they saw the star, how happy they were, what joy was theirs! It went ahead of them until it stopped over the place where the child was. They went into the house, and when they saw the child with his mother Mary, they knelt down and worshipped him. They brought out their gifts of gold, frankincense, and myrrh, and presented them to him.

Matthew 2:9–11

The wise men followed the star to lead them to the baby. They were full of joy to see the baby, and worshipped him. They brought presents, but rather like the star was a sign, so too were the presents. The gold was for a king, the frankincense smelt like the temple and myrrh was used when someone died. Maybe not ideal gifts for every baby but were they right for this special baby?

Prayer jotter

What can I give him,
poor as I am?
If I were a shepherd,
I would bring a lamb.
If I were a wise man,
I would do my part,
But what I can I give him,
give my heart.

From the carol 'In the Bleak Midwinter'

This is a verse from a carol. What does it mean to give Jesus your heart? Draw your present for Jesus.

Waiting

Looking back

Think about the people you live with.

Pray for someone who needs God's help.

Thank God for the person who makes you laugh the most.

To talk about

Do you like waiting?

What do you wait for? A bus, a meal, to be collected, to be old enough to do something, for a birthday or Christmas?

Sometimes waiting can be frustrating, boring and annoying.

Sometimes, if the wait is for something good, it can be exciting.

To do

Tick the things below that you don't mind waiting for and put a cross through the things you hate waiting for.

Explore the Bible

> **At that time there was a man named Simeon living in Jerusalem. He was a good, God-fearing man and was waiting for Israel to be saved. The Holy Spirit was with him and had assured him that he would not die before he had seen the Lord's promised Messiah.**
>
> *Luke 2:25–26*

Simeon was waiting. He had been waiting for years. In fact, he had been waiting all his life. He was waiting to see the person that God would send. (Messiah is another name for Jesus.) The Holy Spirit had told him he would not die until he had. And so he waited.

Prayer jotter

Sometimes we wait, not knowing when the thing will happen. We wait with hope. Simeon hoped for God's Messiah. What do you hope for? Try not to think of things just for you (like presents) but of things for other people.

God's light

Looking back

Are you worried about anything at the moment? God cares about it. Tell him.

What was your best bit of the day just gone? Say thanks!

To talk about

Do you know what you want to be when you grow up?

Is there a particular job you'd like to do or type of person you want to be like?

To do that job, will you need to have special skills or have learnt special things?

To do

Only some adults end up doing what they dreamt of doing as a child. As you meet people who do different jobs, ask them what they wanted to do as a child. Is it the same job?

Explore the Bible

> **Simeon took the child in his arms and gave thanks to God: 'Now, Lord, you have kept your promise, and you may let your servant go in peace. With my own eyes I have seen your salvation, a light to reveal your will to the Gentiles and bring glory to your people Israel.'**
>
> *Luke* 2:28–32

Jesus was going to be a special adult. He was to have a huge effect on the whole of the world and all of history. But he was once just a baby. Simeon held the baby Jesus in his arms and knew that he was going to change the world. Jesus is God's light for the world. Simeon thanks God that he has seen the light with his own eyes.

Prayer jotter

Draw a picture of you doing the job you want to do or being the person you want to be.

Tell God about it in a prayer.

The real child

Looking back

Have you had enough to eat in the last few days? Was it nice food?

Some people don't have enough food. Pray that crops will grow to make food and that rich people will help those who don't have so much.

To talk about

Do you like to see baby animals—kittens, puppies, ducklings? What is your favourite?

They are so small and sweet but they all grow up. When a baby animal grows up, it looks different, but inside it is the same.

To do

Match up the baby with the adult version. Which look most different?

Explore the Bible

> **The child grew and became strong; he was full of wisdom, and God's blessings were upon him.**
>
> *Luke 2:40*

Jesus is just like you and me. He was a baby, grew into a child and then became an adult. He was very special though, even as a child. He was God's son and this verse says that he was full of wisdom. As an adult, he would do amazing things, but remember, he was a real child as well.

Prayer jotter

Re-read what Luke says about Jesus as a child in the Bible verse. Think about what someone might write about you. Write or draw about what you are full of.

For ever there

Looking back

What did you do the last time you were at school?

Think of the best bit and thank God.

Think of the worst bit. Ask God to help it not to happen again or to help you enjoy it more next time.

To talk about

Think about first and last.

What is the first thing you do in the morning?

What is the last thing you do at night?

What is the first letter in the alphabet? What is the last?

What is the first number? Is there a last number?

To do

Link up these pictures with a line, starting with the first one and ending with the last. If you like, you could put in numbers as well.

Explore the Bible

'Listen!' says Jesus. 'I am the first and the last, the beginning and the end.'

Revelation 22:12–13

Here's something amazing about Jesus.

Although he was born as a baby, he was actually around before that. Although he lived on earth as a human about two thousand years ago, his life didn't end with his death. He died but came alive again and is still alive today. Jesus has always been there and always will be for ever more. Wow!

Prayer jotter

Quite a lot of things about God are really difficult for us to understand.

Some things will become clearer as we get older but some things will always be difficult. God is so amazing, but the simplest thing we have to understand is that he loves us.

Talk, write or draw about the difficult things to do with God.

First light

Looking back

Thank God for a happy thing in the day just gone.

Tell God about a sad thing. If you need to, say sorry for it.

To talk about

Look around where you sit. Is it messy or tidy?

Is your chair or bed high or low? Is the room big or little?

How many opposites can you think of, just from looking around the place you are in now?

To do

Match the words to the pictures.

fast - slow, light - dark, high - low, fat - thin

Explore the Bible

> **In the beginning, when God created the universe, the earth was formless and desolate. The raging ocean that covered everything was engulfed in total darkness. Then God commanded, 'Let there be light'—and light appeared.**
>
> *Genesis 1:1–3*

These are the very first verses in the whole Bible. They tell us about two opposite things. They talk of a place that was totally dark. This is what the earth was like before God made the universe. The first thing he made was light—the opposite of darkness.

The second opposite is that the earth used to be formless and desolate. But God gave a command and began to bring order out of chaos.

Prayer jotter

Imagine the earth in the beginning. It was formless and the sea was raging. It was totally dark. Think about the earth now.

Praise God for what he created. Draw or write about creation.

Sun, moon and stars

Looking back

What was the most beautiful thing you saw in the day just gone?

Was it a thing, a place or a person?

Praise God by telling him why you liked it.

To talk about

Do you enjoy making things?

What things have you made? What do you use to make things with?

Butter, sugar, eggs and flour for a cake, plasticine or play dough for models, old boxes for junk modelling?

Most of the things we make are started with something. We make by changing things from one thing into another.

To do

Here's a recipe for very simple biscuits. Get some help and make them sometime.

Using a wooden spoon, mix together 100g butter and 75g sugar. Beat in an egg yolk. Bit by bit, mix in 200g plain flour. Roll out the dough and cut into shapes. Use cutters or the top of a cup. Put on greased baking sheets and cook for ten minutes at Gas Mark 6 (200°C / 400°F).Carefully remove from the oven and sprinkle with sugar. Eat!

Explore the Bible

> **Then God commanded, 'Let lights appear in the sky to separate day from night.' So God made the two larger lights, the sun to rule over the day and the moon to rule over the night; he also made the stars.**
>
> *Genesis 1:14 and 16*

What do you think God started with when he made the sun, moon and stars? Did he make them from flour and eggs? From play dough? No! God made them from nothing! Isn't that amazing? Look up on a dark, clear night and try to count the stars. God made them all—is anything impossible for God?

Prayer jotter

Draw the sun, moon and stars here.

Think about what these lights in the sky do for us.

Say a 'thank you' prayer to God.

God's tent

Looking back

Say thanks to God for your friends.

Tell him why you like them. Ask him to help any who need it.

To talk about

What is the biggest thing you've seen?

Is it a building? An animal? A bus or lorry?

How big is the sea? How far does the sky go?

Are they bigger than a skyscraper or a whale?

To do

Put these things in size order, either with a line to link them or with numbers.

Explore the Bible

> **Praise the Lord, my soul! O Lord, my God, how great you are! You are clothed with majesty and glory; you cover yourself with light. You have spread out the heavens like a tent and built your home on the waters above.**
>
> *Psalm 104:1–3*

These Bible verses help us begin to imagine how big God is. However, I don't think we'll ever really understand! It says that the heavens are like a tent for God. Wow! That's a big tent! Next time you look up at the sky, think about it as God's tent.

Prayer jotter

God's size is impossible for us to describe. No person will ever know.

'O Lord, my God, how great you are!' says the Bible verse.

Think about the really huge things and about how much bigger God is than them. Write or draw them here.

Crowned in glory

Looking back

What is your favourite food? Say thanks to God that you can taste it and enjoy it.

Ask God to help those people without enough food.

To talk about

Think of the smallest thing you know of.

What is it? An insect? A grain of sand?

Have you ever used a magnifying glass or microscope?

How much can you see with one?

To do

Look at the tip of your finger now. What can you see?

Now look really closely. Can you see any more?

Now use a bright light. Does that help you to see more?

If you have a magnifying glass, use that. What else can you see now?

Explore the Bible

> **When I look at the sky, which you have made, at the moon and the stars, which you set in their places—what are human beings, that you think of them; mere mortals, that you care for them?**
>
> **Yet you made them inferior only to yourself; you crowned them with glory and honour.**
>
> *Psalm 8:3–5*

Isn't it amazing that even though we are so small compared to God, still he cares for us? He knows us all. He even knows how many lines you have on your fingertip. In fact, not only does he care for and know us, he has also crowned us with glory. We are so special that we are like God's royal family.

Prayer jotter

If God is so big and we are so small, how can we be special enough to be crowned by God? I don't know, but we are!

Praise and thank God in a written or drawn prayer.

No more sunshine

Looking back

Have you done anything naughty in the last few days?

Did you hurt or upset anyone else? Did it upset God?

If you haven't done so already, say sorry to God.

To talk about

Do you like sunny days? Why?

You can play outside and it feels warm.

Have you ever been to a place sunnier than where you live now?

What was it like?

To do

Circle the things here which are for sunny days.

Explore the Bible

Then I saw a new heaven and a new earth. The first heaven and the first earth disappeared, and the sea vanished. The city has no need of the sun or the moon to shine on it, because the glory of God shines on it, and the Lamb is its lamp.

Revelation 21:1, 23

The Bible tells us that one day God will change this earth and create a new heaven and a new earth. This will be more amazing and more perfect than what we know today. In that new place, there won't be a need for the sun or the moon because God's glory will shine so brightly. The Lamb is another name for Jesus and he will be the lamp for the city, shining brightly, guiding people around.

Prayer jotter

In the new heaven and earth, God will be with us in a new way and we will be his people. Imagine what it will be like to meet God, who will be as bright as the sun.

Write or draw about it here.

Week 4
Session 6

Star Jesus

Looking back

What do you enjoy doing the most at the moment?

Tell God about it. Thank him that you are able to do it.

To talk about

Very occasionally you can see just one star in the daylight sky. More often, but still rarely, you can see the moon even though it's daytime.

What do you think that looks like? Bright, pale, large, small?

To do

One day, maybe during the summer holidays, get up in time to see the dawn. You will probably need someone to wake you up and be with you, and it will need to be nice weather, so plan in advance! What does the rising sun look like? What colour is the sky? What do you hear?

Explore the Bible

> **'I, Jesus, am the bright morning star.'**
>
> *Revelation 22:16*

The bright morning star is yet another picture-name given to Jesus. One thing it means is that he is the beginning of a new day, like dawn-time. He is like a bright star in a big sky, pointing forwards into new things.

Prayer jotter

A new day is a new beginning. Is there anything you would like Jesus to help you start again? Tell him about it here, in words or pictures.

World light

Looking back

What sound do you most like to hear? Maybe your ears don't work very well—can you feel noises?

Think of the nicest or best noises you know, and thank God for them.

To talk about

When it's night-time and dark, what things help us to see better? What do we have indoors that helps us? What about outdoors? In the street?

What helps things to be seen better?

What do we do so that we are seen in the dark?

To do

Find things that help us to see and be seen in the dark—a torch, a reflective strip (look on trainers, a clock with luminous hands or bike reflectors). Put them in a dark place and look at them working.

Explore the Bible

> **Jesus spoke to the Pharisees again. 'I am the light of the world,' he said. 'Whoever follows me will have the light of life and will never walk in darkness.'**
>
> *John 8:12*

Jesus is the light for the whole world. This means that he will guide us through life. Sometimes he feels far away—but he is there, and because he is the light he can even be seen in the dark, if we know where to look.

Prayer jotter

Jesus wants to help and guide us in life, like a lamp or torch guides us at night.

What do you need a guide for now? Tell Jesus about it.

Shining light

Looking back

Is there anyone you know who is not well?

Ask God to take away any pain or discomfort they might have.

Who needs to know God's love today? Pray for them.

To talk about

Has anyone ever been nasty to you? How did it feel?

Has anyone been mean to someone special to you?

Did it hurt you too?

Have you ever listened to or watched the news and seen the horrible things that happen to people all over the world?

To do

Here are some things that would cheer up someone who had been upset. What would you choose for whom?

Explore the Bible

> **The Word was the source of life, and this life brought light to humanity. The light shines in the darkness, and the darkness has never put it out.**
>
> *John 1:4–5*

The Bible says that when people do wrong things it is as if they are in darkness. Often, when it's you who have been hurt, it feels like you are in the dark too. But Jesus is the light, and he promises that no amount of wrong things (darkness) can ever put his light out.

Prayer jotter

When you are upset by someone, look to Jesus to give you reassurance that things will be OK. When you're hurting, imagine Jesus giving you a big smile or a hug.

Draw Jesus as the light here.

God is light

Looking back

Do you know anyone who lives in another country?

Pray for them now.

To talk about

Have you ever opened up a new pot of paint? What colour was it?

Was there any other colour in it or was it completely pure?

Do you like starting a clean page in your books at school?

What is that like? Do you like it because the page is so clean and untouched?

What happens to the paint when someone dabs in a paintbrush that they haven't washed?

What happens to that clean page when you make a mistake on it?

To do

What has happened to these things?

Explore the Bible

> **God is light and there is no darkness at all in him.**
>
> *1 John 1:5*

When the Bible says that God is light, it means that he is completely pure and holy. This means that he is completely unspoilt by anything impure or unholy. We have seen that darkness is like a picture of the things people do wrong (we call this 'sin').

Unlike fresh paint that gets spoilt by a dirty paintbrush, or a clean floor that gets dirt on it from muddy feet, God is completely untouched by anything that could spoil him.

God is unspoilt by sin because there is no darkness in him.

Prayer jotter

God promises to forgive us when we say sorry for our sins. Imagine that our sin is like a stain on our clothes. When we are forgiven by God, it's as if he gives us clean clothes.

Say sorry to God for wrong things you did today and then draw yourself in your new, 'forgiven clothes'.

Week 5
Session 4

Heart light

Looking back

Who needs God's help at the moment? Tell their name to God.

Is there anything you need to say sorry to God for?

To talk about

Do you know anyone who wears a uniform? What job are they doing?

Why do you think they wear a uniform?

Have you ever seen a play or seen a TV show where people dress up in funny clothes?

Why do they dress up?

What does it help us to understand about the story?

To do

If you saw any of these things, what would you know about the person who owned them?

Explore the Bible

The God who said, 'Out of darkness the light shall shine!' is the same God who made his light shine in our hearts, to bring us the knowledge of God's glory shining in the face of Christ.

2 Corinthians 4:6

We know what some people do by what they wear. Some people show us what they like by what they carry. Some people are actors and pretend to be someone else to make a play as real as possible.

God wants us to be known as his friends. Rather than giving us something to wear or carry, he has put his light in our hearts. Whenever we try to be like Jesus, that light shines on to others and they see God in us.

Prayer jotter

God has promised to put his light in our hearts. We can believe that God's promises are true because all through the Bible his promises come true. We say that God is 'faithful' to us.

Thank God that his promise to put a light in our heart is true. Draw yourself with a heart light.

Show your light

Looking back

Pray for your school.

Is there a part of school life that needs God's help? Ask him for that.

To talk about

Is it easy or hard to cut off light completely?

How could you make it totally dark in your room?

If you were to go outside your house at night-time, would you be able to see your light, even through the curtains?

To do

Is it possible to hide light?

Try to find somewhere in your room where all the light is cut out. Even the crack of light under the door! Even the little light shining through the duvet!

Explore the Bible

'You are like light for the whole world. No one lights a lamp and puts it under a bowl; instead he puts it on the lampstand, where it gives light for everyone in the house. In the same way your light must shine before people, so that they will see the good things you do and praise your Father in heaven.'

Matthew 5:14–16

Jesus was talking to his friends when he said these words. Being a friend of Jesus makes us a light in the darkness of the world. We mustn't hide our light, says Jesus. He means that we mustn't pretend we don't know who Jesus is. We must let our friends know that Jesus is our light.

Prayer jotter

Sometimes it is hard to tell others about Jesus, especially if our friends think it's silly. It's probably because they don't understand what he is like.

Pray, using this space, that you will be a shining light for God.

Week 5
Session 6

You are a star!

Looking back

Look at your things around you. Pray for children around the world who have no toys or nice things. Ask God to be with them.

To talk about

Do you know anybody who is a fan of something? Football fans, fans of a pop group or perhaps a fan of a game or hobby? Have you seen the things that they have ?

A fisherman has a rod and net, a cook has an apron and cookbooks.

What fans do you know? What things do they have?

Have you noticed how much they talk about the thing they like, as well?

To do

Match the fan to their things.

Explore the Bible

Do everything without complaining or arguing. You must shine among people like stars lighting up the sky, as you offer them the message of life.

Philippians 2:14–16

We can be a fan of Jesus! We can collect the kit and go to meetings! But what Jesus wants is for us to try to be *like* him. This verse says that we need to try to be really polite and kind, so that people will see we are different because we know Jesus. In that way we will shine like a star in a dark night sky. Then, people will notice us and wonder what makes us different.

Prayer jotter

How big a fan of Jesus are you? What things can you do to show others that Jesus is in your life?

Say thank you to God for all the ways that he has helped you to be a star, and ask him to help you get better at shining.